How to
Read a US
Roadmap

Robert C.A. Goff

Dreamsplice
Christiansburg, Virginia

How to Read a US Roadmap

Image credits on page 4.

Dreamsplice
3462 Dairy Road
Christiansburg, VA 24073

www.dreamsplice.com/books

Cover design by Robert C.A. Goff, Copyright © 2019 by Dreamsplice

ISBN: 978-1-7333979-0-2
Library of Congress Control Number:2019911376

First Edition: September 2019

TABLE of CONTENTS

Image Credits

[Listed by source alphabetically, with page on which it is presented, and image position on that page. Their respective copyrights and trademarks apply. Some have been overlaid with conspicuous arrows and notes for clarification. All map images are included for their instructional value.]

Alabama Dept of Transportation
> 47b

DeLorme
> back cover image, 6, 9d, 23b1, 23d1, 28c

Michelin North America, Inc.
> 31a1, 31c1, 31c2

Nevada Dept of Transportation
> 24

Oklahoma Dept of Transportation
> 27c2, 27d, 28a, 28b

Robert Teeple Petley
> 40a

Rand McNally
> front cover image, 6, 9a, 9b, 9c, 15a, 19a2, 19b, 19c, 19d, 23c, 27c1, 35b2, 39a, 39b, 39c, 39d, 47a, 47c, 47d, 48, 51a, 51b

Southeast Publications USA Inc.
> 11a, 11b, 40b1, 40b2

US Forest Service
> 6, 11c, 15b, 19a1, 20, 27a, 27b

US Geological Survey (USGS)
> 6, 11d, 32, 35b1, 35d, 43b

https://www.daz3d.com/aako
> 43d

All other images are by the author.

Why Learn to Read a Roadmap?

Learning to read a roadmap is a basic skill that will reassure you when you venture into unfamiliar areas. In addition to serving as an energy-free backup for digital mapping devices, roadmaps allow you to orient yourself to your surroundings, and provide you with the geographic *context* of where you choose to travel.

A printed map or atlas can be marked-up with a ballpoint pen or highlighted with a marker. Maps of special trips can be hung on the wall.

In the recent past, printed maps were everywhere. Gasoline service stations gave them away for free. Every new driver learned quickly how to interpret the roadmaps for places they traveled.

For over a generation, digital mapping devices and software have gradually displaced paper maps. The dozens of unique symbols used on roadmaps for nearly a century may now be a puzzle to some drivers.

One remarkable advantage of a paper map is that it enables a curious traveler to see what might be out there, rather than just entering a starting point and an endpoint.

> *Devices, computers and applications that depend on Internet connectivity sometimes become unavailable at truly inconvenient times.*

And in some situations, GPS routing may not be the wisest or even the easiest or fastest route to follow.

2020
Road Atlas
RAND McNALLY
LARGE SCALE
35% Larger Map
than the regular Road Atlas maps
America's #1 Road Atlas
VIRGINIA
ATLAS & GAZETTEER
THE ATLAS
Index
Legend of Map Symbols
Topographic Road Maps
Pages 2–4
Inside Front Cover
Pages 18–80
Grand Canyon
National Park
207
GEOGRAPHIC MAPS
ILLUSTRATED
DETAILED
LOCATER MAP
BACK OF ATLAS
THE GAZETTEER
ence Centers
as
rips
PAGE(S)
14–15
Kaibab
National Forest
North Kaibab Ranger District
$8.99

Kinds of Roadmaps

This book is about reading roadmaps in the United States. Maps from other parts of the world are generally similar, though the distance units and many of the symbols used may differ.

While most types of "roadmaps" can assist you in getting where you want to go, selecting the best map for your needs makes it easier.

For long-distance driving, a map of an entire state or group of states will focus on major highways—Interstate highways, US highways and other major roads. A road atlas of many state maps may be perfect for road trips of several hundred to several thousand miles.

For the glove box of your car or truck, a folded map of your state is a good insurance policy. If you live or travel mostly at the boundary of several states, then a map of each of those states should be in there.

A dedicated city map will always provide better details of a city than the city "inset" on a larger map. City maps usually indicate one-way streets, the access roads to major academic, cultural and sports locations, and maybe street address ranges.

Are you off to drive the country back roads? A county map showing both paved and unpaved roads, and possibly the lay and steepness of the land (topographical features) will reveal the greatest opportunities for exploration.

National Parks and National Forests often offer their own detailed maps of roads, sights and trails. And for serious hiking and backpacking, a dedicated topographical map from the US Geological Survey (USGS) is ideal. These come in various scales, to show lesser or greater levels of detail.

Of course, if you are visiting a tourist area, a "tourist" map will include points of interest and tourism-related businesses. These may not accurately show the distances and precise locations.

An atlas of maps 
These can be nationwide in scope, or restricted to a single state or group of states. The printing format may range from a small handbook to a large, spiral-bound behemoth.

The Large Scale Rand McNally US Road Atlas is the easiest to read, and can open to lay flat. It can even be folded open onto itself, so it is easier to hold while viewing a single page.

Maps of major highways and some minor roads 
Roads suitable for getting you from one city or town to another are usually the only roads shown on a "highway" roadmap. There is seldom detail of city streets, other than the main thoroughfares. But these maps often display other helpful information, such as distances, travel times, Interstate exit numbers, and whether or not there is a toll (a fee) for driving on a particular road.

City street maps 
For medium to larger size cities, a detailed city map offers block-by-block street names, one-way streets, significant locations (such as museums, universities, parks, sports arenas, parking garages and cemeteries) and sometimes include street address number ranges for each segment of a street. They may also provide routing for public transportation (buses, subways, etc.).

County and topographical roadmaps 
In addition to major roads, county and topographical ("topo") maps will reveal many of the minor roads, whether paved or unpaved. Some county maps are "flat", while others—the topo maps—include indicators of the lay of the land and steepness of the terrain.

RAND McNALLY
2020
Road Atlas
LARGE SCALE 35% Larger Maps
than the regular Road Atlas maps

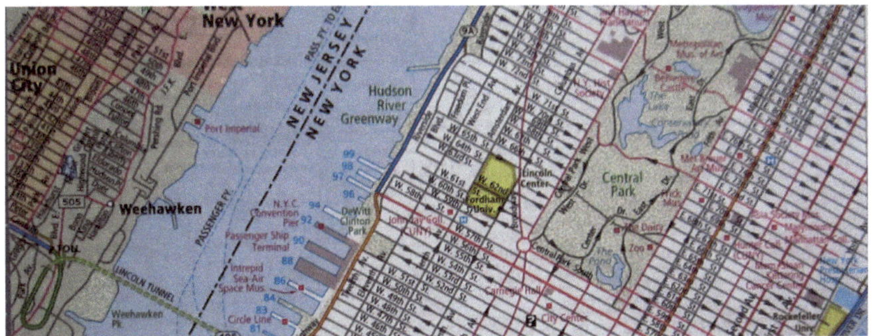

Tourist maps 

These handy maps are often not drawn to scale. Their purpose is to highlight locations specifically of interest to tourists, and to show major road connections and nearby cities and some towns.

Advertiser maps 

Advertiser maps are offered to local businesses, in exchange for (sometimes) exclusive advertising of their particular kinds of businesses. If advertisers purchase an ad, their direct competitors cannot. The map graphic is surrounded by ads, each containing a letter or number key for its location on the adjoining map.

Forest Service maps 

These maps are primarily for showing roads that exist within a National Forest. These roads are often unpaved, and not well maintained. High clearance (SUV) and possibly four-wheel drive may be needed. If the area includes a town or village, then the paved roads are shown as well.

US Geological Survey (USGS) maps 

USGS topographical maps attempt to show everything. They map paved roads, unpaved roads and even paths and trails. They show the lay of the land with "contour lines"—brown, squiggly lines indicating elevation. When the contour lines are far apart, the slope is gradual or flat. When the contour lines are close together, then the terrain is quite steep. They are always drawn to an accurate scale, shown in the map legend.

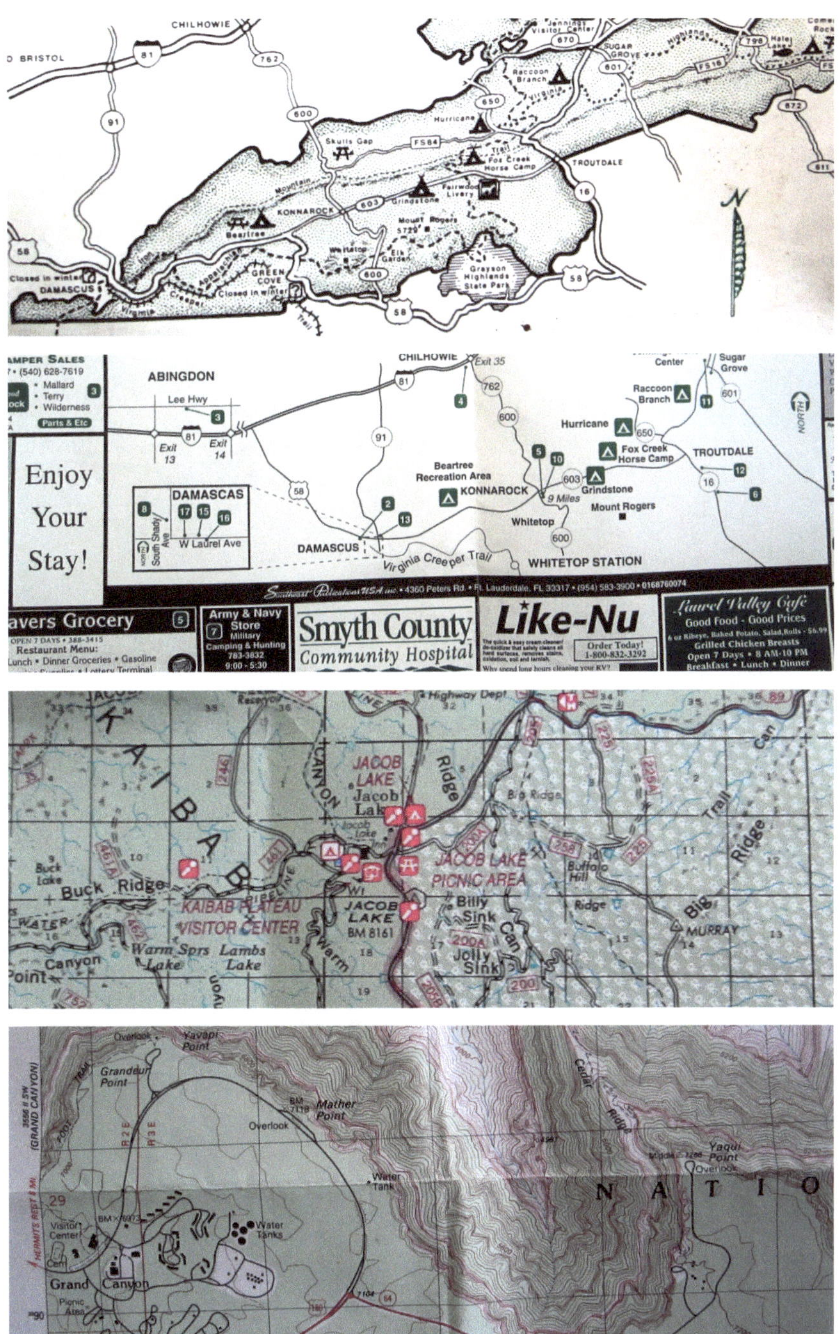
CHILHOWIE
BRISTOL
SUGAR GROVE
Raccoon Branch
TROUTDALE
Skulls Gap
Fox Creek Horse Camp
Fairwood Livery
KONNAROCK
Grindstone
Mount Rogers 5729'
Beartree
Whitetop
Elk Garden
GREEN COVE
Grayson Highlands State Park
Closed in winter
DAMASCUS
Appalachian Trail
Virginia Creeper Trail
Closed in winter
N

CAMPER SALES
(540) 628-7619
Mallard
Terry
Wilderness
Parts & Etc
ABINGDON
CHILHOWIE
Exit 35
Lee Hwy
Exit 13
Exit 14
Enjoy Your Stay!
DAMASCAS
South Shady Ave
W Laurel Ave
DAMASCUS
Beartree Recreation Area
KONNAROCK
9 Miles
Whitetop
Hurricane
Fox Creek Horse Camp
Grindstone
Mount Rogers
Center
Sugar Grove
Raccoon Branch
TROUTDALE
Virginia Creeper Trail
WHITETOP STATION
Smithwest Publications USA Inc. • 4360 Peters Rd. • Ft. Lauderdale, FL 33317 • (954) 583-3900 • 0168760074

avers Grocery
OPEN 7 DAYS • 388-3415
Restaurant Menu:
Lunch • Dinner Groceries • Gasoline
Army & Navy Store
Military Camping & Hunting
783-3632
9:00 - 5:30
Smyth County Community Hospital
Like-Nu
Order Today!
1-800-832-3292
Laurel Valley Cafe
Good Food - Good Prices
Grilled Chicken Breasts
Open 7 Days • 8 AM-10 PM
Breakfast • Lunch • Dinner

KAIBAB
JACOB LAKE
Jacob Lake
Big Ridge
JACOB LAKE PICNIC AREA
Buffalo Hill
Trail
Ridge
Buck Ridge
KAIBAB PLATEAU VISITOR CENTER
JACOB LAKE
BM 8161
Billy Sink
MURRAY
WATER
Warm Sprs Lambs Lake
Jolly Sink
Canyon Point

Overlook
Yavapi Point
Grandeur Point
Mather Point
Overlook
Cedar Ridge
Yaqui Point
Overlook
(GRAND CANYON)
HERMITS REST 8 MI
Visitor Center
Water Tank
Water Tanks
NATIO
Grand Canyon
Picnic Area
Campground

Be sure someone knows where you plan to go and when you expect to return, if you wander down a Forest Service road.

Orient the Map

Global Positioning Satellite (GPS) devices know where you are, and usually know which direction you are facing or heading. A printed map, by contrast, knows nothing about where you are located or which direction you are facing or heading. It's just sitting on the table or your lap, oriented however you happened to place it there.

For most maps, though not all, the **top of the map** is compass North. This is often indicated by a printed "compass rose" that includes a pointer or arrow pointing toward a large letter "N" or the word "North". Maps that are rotated otherwise, in order to fit the mapped area onto a rectangular sheet of paper, will usually indicate that rotation with a compass rose, so you know which way is North on the map.

After looking at the map, then looking out at your surroundings, which direction in the real world is North? The act of rotating your map's North to face the real world's North is called "orienting the map".

If you happen to have a **compass** (any cheap one will do, and you can just toss it into your glove box), you simply lay your compass onto the map, with its North marking aligned with the North of the map's compass rose, then rotate the map until the compass *needle* points North. The map is now oriented to the real world. If there are nearby landmarks (towns or intersections or peaks) shown on the map, they should be visible at those locations in the real world about you.

If you find yourself without a compass, there are a number of methods for figuring out which way is North. Some highway road signs indicate the general compass direction. The **sun** rises in the East, and sets in the West. At night, learn to identify the **North Star**. **Constellation**s (and the **moon**) rise in the East and set in the West.

During the day, **a stick in the ground** will cast a shadow that moves as time passes. Mark the tip of the **shadow**, then repeat in an hour or more to define an East-West line.

Point the hour hand of a **watch** at the sun. Halfway between that time and "12" is South.

The top is usually North 

If a map does not have a compass rose, it is usually safe to assume that North is at the top of the map when the words on the map are right side up. Compass roses are often quite decorative, and look different on maps from different publishers. It can be as simple as a thin, straight arrow with "N" at the tip, or can be more elaborate, with corporate logos embedded.

Compass 

Topographical maps, especially those from the USGS or Forest Service, may show a compass rose that is actually a compass. Since magnetic north (in most locations in the US) is not exactly true North, a correction may also be indicated. This correction is called *declination*. If you are **on foot**, and crossing unmarked terrain, then declination is important. For following a road in a car, you can safely ignore declination.

Road signs 

Most highways in the US are said to be north-south or east-west. Even highways that are not aligned that way are still marked that way. Sometimes this designated alignment is shown on the road signs for the route numbers.

Daytime gimmick 

This watch trick only works if 1) you wear a watch, 2) it is an analog watch, with hands, and 3) you can figure out where the sun is positioned along the horizon. (You don't point the hour hand up into the sky.) Also, *you need to use Standard Time*. If the watch is set to Daylight Savings Time, then pretend the hour hand is positioned an hour earlier. [If it says 3 daylight time, then point 2 O'clock at the location of the sun over the horizon.]

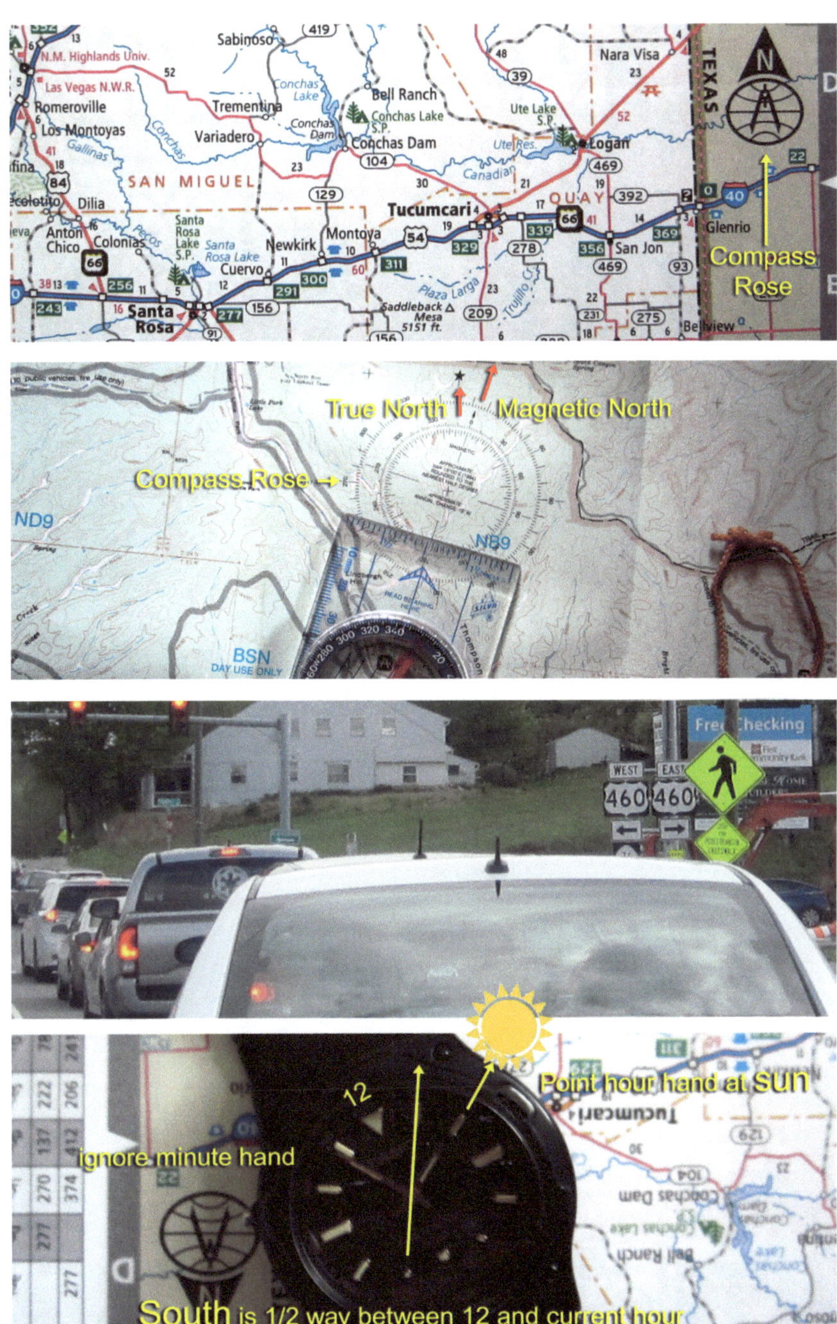
Compass Rose
True North   Magnetic North
Compass Rose →
Point hour hand at Sun
ignore minute hand
12
South is 1/2 way between 12 and current hour

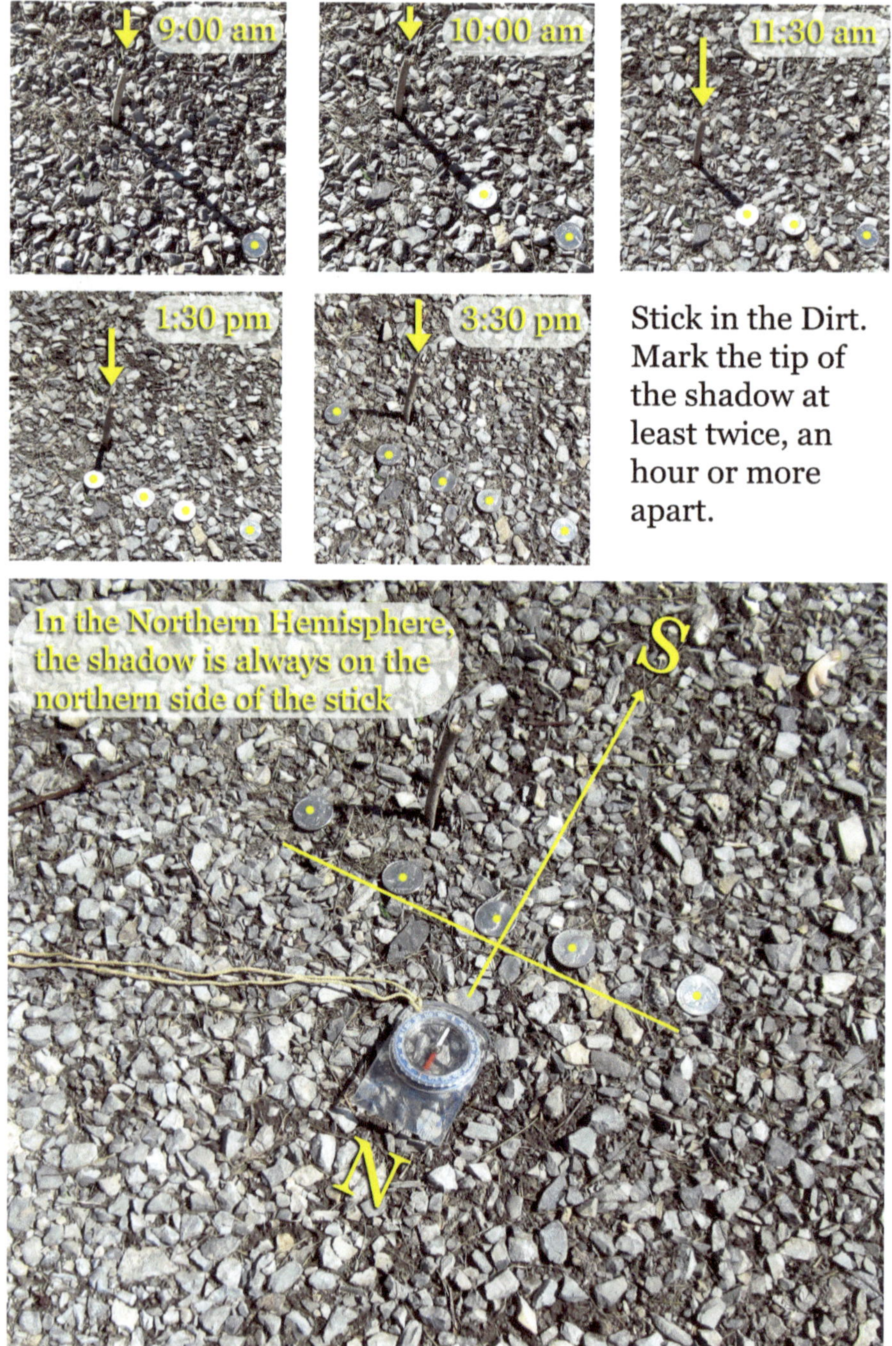

Stick in the Dirt. Mark the tip of the shadow at least twice, an hour or more apart.

Mark the tip of a shadow cast by a stick, using coins or pebbles. The line runs from W. to E. Shadow is North of the stick.

Map Legend and Index

Somewhere on every map, there is a "legend" that has a statement of when the map was published (the copyright date). There is often a lot of other useful information in the legend. The legend is where you will find the **scale** of the map (such as "1 inch = 5 miles"), a **bar scale** (a small "ruler" for measuring distances on the map), definitions of **symbols** used on the map (such as a primary road vs. a secondary or minor road), and who or what organization or company published the map.

Checking the publication date of a map will tell you whether or not it is out of date. While cities and towns and mountains don't move, new roads certainly are constructed from time to time, and some maps may also show stretches of roads that are under construction or "proposed" for construction in the future. Short-term detours are usually not shown on maps.

Most maps of very small areas don't contain an **index**. It's easy enough to locate what you might be looking for. Maps of larger areas may provide an index of cities and towns and other locations of interest.

A typical index will be listed alphabetically, and may indicate a population for towns and cities, as well as **map coordinates** for locating that item on the map. These coordinates correspond to numbers and letters along the edges of the map. So if, for example, a town is stated to be at "C-9", then you locate "C" on the margin of the map, locate "9" on the adjacent margin, and follow these two coordinates to where they intersect. The town will be somewhere within that rectangle.

Symbols may vary from one kind of map to another. Similar kinds of maps from different publishers may use different symbols, but the most commonly used symbols are fairly standard on all maps. Be sure to understand which kinds of lines represent which kinds of roads (Interstate highways, US highways, multi-lane roads, limited access roads, rural roads).

A limited access road is designed for heavy through traffic. There are no driveway or business entrances, no traffic lights, and no intersections. Interstate highways are designed that way. You can enter or exit only at designated places, and crossing roads go either under it or over it.

Publication date: is it out of date? 

The map shown with 2019 as its publication date prominently says, "2020" on the cover. Since it was published in April of 2019, its mapping data was gathered mostly in 2018.

The legend of the (now out of date) Forest Service map actually gives a detailed history of when it was created and subsequently updated.

What's in an index? 

A map index lists cities and towns and important locations, along with *where to find them on the map.*

This index from a Rand McNally Road Atlas shows that a location in Oklahoma called Camp Houston is located at map coordinates "C-9".   Camp Houston shows no population information, but other nearby entries do. (Duncan, OK has a population of 23,431 people.)

Horizontal and vertical locations (map coordinates) 

In our index listing for Camp Houston, OK, we were told that we can find it at map coordinates "C-9". There is a "C" located in both margins at the *sides* of the map, and there is a "9" located in the margins at the *top* and *bottom* of the map. Where "C" intersects with "9", we discover Camp Houston (yellow circle) up in the corner of that rectangle (yellow shading).

Symbols 

The partial list of symbols shown are useful in determining what *kind* of roads are represented by which *kinds* of map lines. The difference between limited access *toll roads* and those that do not charge a fee is indicated by a different color line.

The heavy, dashed green line means maybe there is a road there today; maybe not.

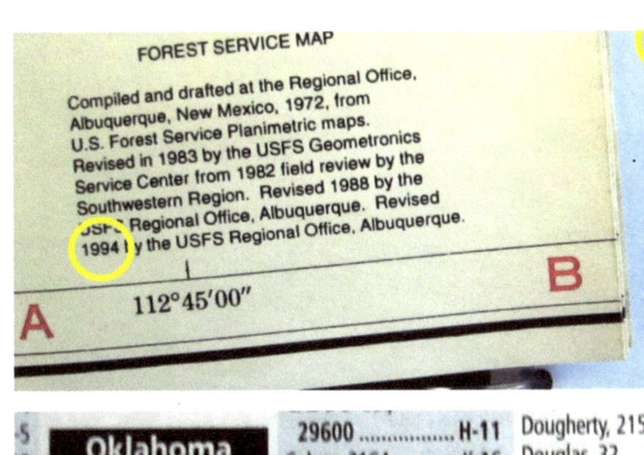
FOREST SERVICE MAP
Compiled and drafted at the Regional Office,
Albuquerque, New Mexico, 1972, from
U.S. Forest Service Planimetric maps.
Revised in 1983 by the USFS Geometronics
Service Center from 1982 field review by the
Southwestern Region. Revised 1988 by the
USFS Regional Office, Albuquerque. Revised
1994 by the USFS Regional Office, Albuquerque.
112°45'00"
A
B
©2019 RM Acquisition, LLC d/b/a
Rand McNally. Rand McNally, the
globe logo, and Always Gets You
There are registered trademarks of
RM Acquisition, LLC. All other
trademarks appearing in this
publication are trademarks of third
parties and are the responsibility of
their respective owners.
For licensing information and
copyright permissions, contact us at
permissions@randmcnally.com.
If you have a comment, suggestion,
or even a compliment, please
visit us at randmcnally.com/contact

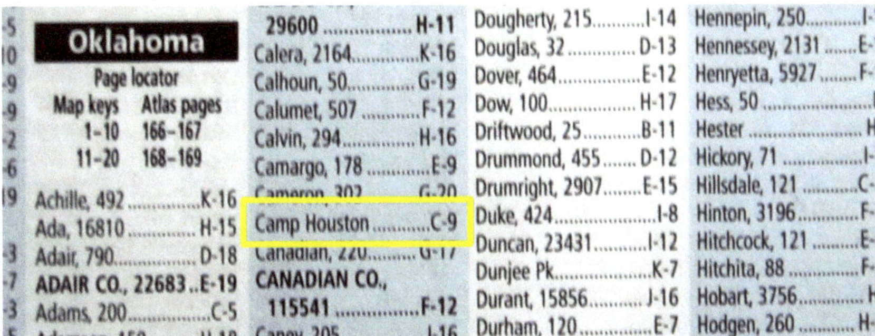
Oklahoma
Page locator
Map keys   Atlas pages
1–10   166–167
11–20   168–169

Achille, 492 ....K-16
Ada, 16810 ....H-15
Adair, 790 ....D-18
ADAIR CO., 22683..E-19
Adams, 200..................C-5
Adamson, 150   H-18

29600 .... H-11
Calera, 2164.............K-16
Calhoun, 50...........G-19
Calumet, 507 ....F-12
Calvin, 294...............H-16
Camargo, 178 ....E-9
Cameron, 303   G-20
Camp Houston C-9
Canadian, 220.........G-17
CANADIAN CO.,
115541 ....F-12
Caney, 205   I-16

Dougherty, 215...........I-14
Douglas, 32 ....D-13
Dover, 464.................E-12
Dow, 100.................H-17
Driftwood, 25............B-11
Drummond, 455.......D-12
Drumright, 2907........E-15
Duke, 424.....................I-8
Duncan, 23431...........I-12
Dunjee Pk.................K-7
Durant, 15856...........J-16
Durham, 120.............E-7

Hennepin, 250............I-
Hennessey, 2131 ....E-
Henryetta, 5927 ....F-
Hess, 50 ....
Hester ....H
Hickory, 71 ....I-
Hillsdale, 121 ....C-
Hinton, 3196...........F-
Hitchcock, 121 ....E-
Hitchita, 88 ....F-
Hobart, 3756...........H
Hodgen, 260 ....H-

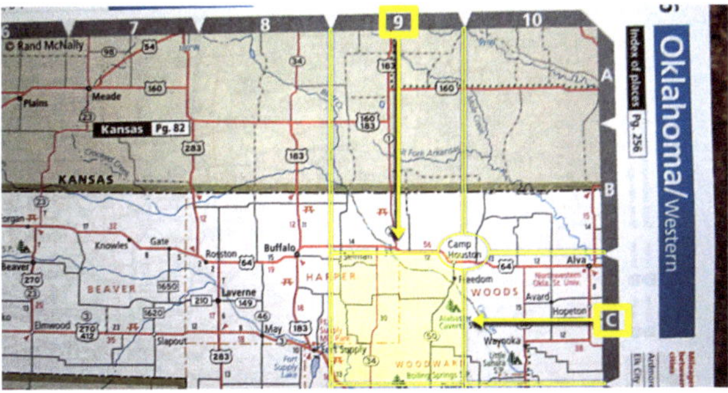
Oklahoma/Western
Index of places Pg. 256
Rand McNally
Kansas Pg. 82
KANSAS
Plains
Meade
Knowles Gate
Buffalo
Rosston
Camp Houston
Alva
Freedom
BEAVER
HARPER
Northwestern Okla. St. Univ.
WOODS
Laverne
May
Avard
Hopeton
Beaver
Elmwood
Slapout
Fort Supply Lake
Waynoka
WOODWARD
Little Sahara

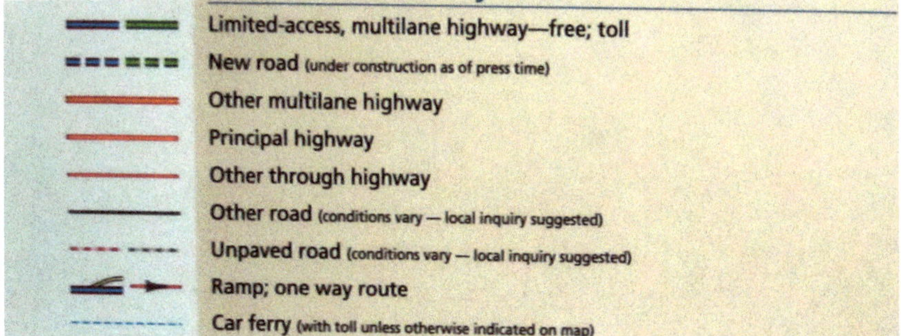
Limited-access, multilane highway—free; toll
New road (under construction as of press time)
Other multilane highway
Principal highway
Other through highway
Other road (conditions vary — local inquiry suggested)
Unpaved road (conditions vary — local inquiry suggested)
Ramp; one way route
Car ferry (with toll unless otherwise indicated on map)

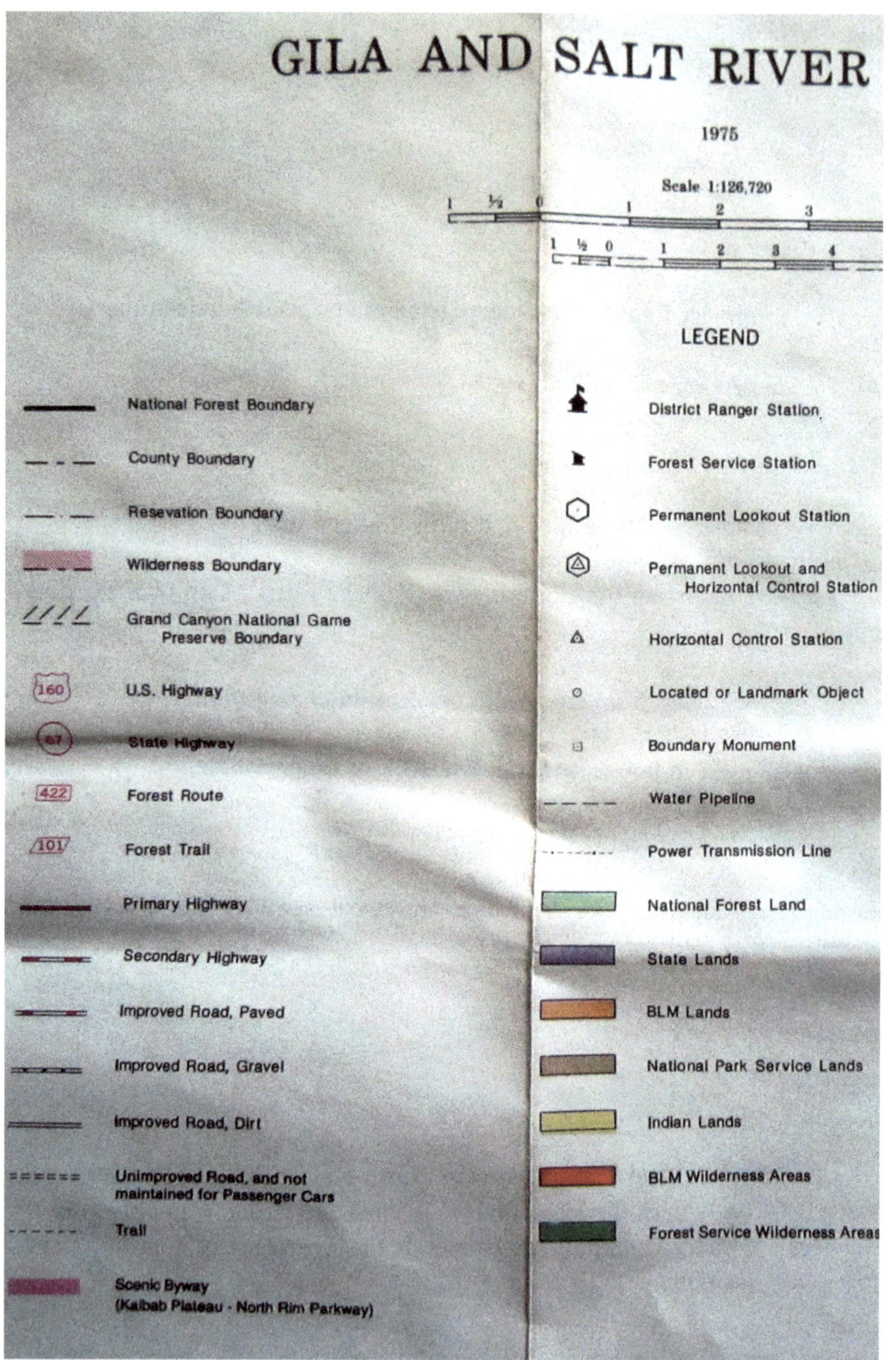

Every map style and publisher may use different symbols.

Boundaries and Colors

Although maps intended for geography ("Can you locate Idaho?") use a variety of **colors** to easily separate and identify states or countries, roadmaps generally use a white or light background *for the area of interest*. So a roadmap map of, say Alabama, will likely use a primarily white background, while the adjacent states will use a background of a darker color. This makes the state boundary obvious.

A white background allows the lines used for the various types of roads to stand out. It also allows special areas, like State Forests and National Forests and Parks to be shaded in a contrasting color, often a light green. Since all the tiny, colored symbols for other locations (rest areas, highway exits, small towns, historic sites, airports and military bases) are important to the meaning of roadmaps, a white background allows them to be easily recognized.

Larger towns and cities are often shaded in a distinct color, so that their boundaries are clear.

Broken lines (dashes or alternating dash-dot, etc.) indicate political boundaries that represent national boundaries, Native tribal land boundaries, state boundaries and county boundaries within each state.   While driving, a national boundary is impossible to miss, since there may be a customs station on either side of the boundary, and you will most likely be required to stop, and present identification papers.

Since states in the US independently decide on their driving laws, state boundaries are often well marked by large road signs, together with smaller signs that may announce abrupt changes in law, like a different speed limit, different restrictions on seat belt use and child restraint requirements, and perhaps local and state emergency phone numbers, road-condition radio stations, and even websites related to traffic and weather conditions.

County lines are often crossed without the slightest thought. They are often marked with only a tiny sign, and seldom present any changes in applicable laws. (Certain counties in some states post that alcoholic drinks are not allowed within their county.)

City limits 

Many cities and towns display an impressive, artistic sign at points where major roads enter. These are sometimes placed not at the actual boundary, but at a point inside or outside the boundary by as much as a half-mile, so as to increase visibility to drivers, or occasionally because of donated land for a large sign. There is usually a small, text road sign at the actual boundary.

On roadmaps, city and town boundaries may be vague.

County lines 

The county boundaries on most maps are more or less conspicuous. In this example, it is shown as a yellow highlight over a broken line on the map.

By contrast, the real life boundary of the counties in this example is marked along the road as a barely noticeable, two-foot-wide road sign that can easily be missed, even if you care to find it.

State boundaries 

State boundaries are always well marked on roadmaps, and that is important. Within the US, state governments decide on the rules and laws for driving in their own states. So when you cross a state boundary, the motor vehicle laws will likely be different from the one state to the next. That also means that seat belt laws may be different, and *the speed limit may suddenly change as you cross into a new state.*

Parks, forests, special areas 

In the topo map on the left, the diagonal band of green is all Jefferson National Forest, but you won't pass the large sign for the National Forest (in this example) until you have driven nearly halfway across the forest. Much smaller, inconspicuous road signs for the actual boundaries can be found at either edge of the forest along this highway, but you would need to look carefully for them in order to spot them.

WELCOME TO RADFORD
HEART OF THE NEW RIVER VALLEY
ENTER FLOYD CO LEAVE MONTGOMERY CO
JEFFERSON National Forest
Sign

Every mile, and often every tenth of a mile is marked by at least a small road sign on Interstate highways. Exits are numbered by their mile marker nearest a whole mile.

Distances and Mileage Charts

The map distance between two points can be measured with a ruler. But that gives you the distance "as the crow flies". That distance will not give you the *driving distance,* unless you are traveling on a perfectly straight road between two points.

What a driver (as opposed to a crow) wants to know is how far is it along the roads that I must travel. This *driving distance* is the distance that is shown on roadmaps, in tiny numbers alongside the line of the roads on the map, as well as in lookup tables and on special "driving distance" maps, which don't actually show roads, but straight lines that indicate the driving distance on the *likely* route between two major cities, as well as an estimated *driving time.*

What do these two numbers mean? The driving distance is fairly accurate, if you drive on the primary roads connecting the two points, but underestimate the distance if you decide to follow a more "scenic" route.

The driving *time* is never accurate. Your actual driving time depends on the speed at which you are driving, and the burden of traffic on the road—which in turn depends on the time of day. Driving time is increased during busy traffic times, especially in urban areas during "rush hours" in the morning and evening, when large numbers of vehicles are traveling between work and home.

Driving time is sometimes slowed by rain or high winds or icy conditions or snow. And temporary road work may require detours that will not appear on your roadmap.

There is also the curious "inaccuracy" of your vehicle's speedometer. Virtually no speedometer displays your actual speed. When it displays 70 mph, for example, you may really be traveling at only 65 mph or 67 mph. Due to the inaccuracy of the measurement of speed (new tires rotate fewer times to go the same distance as worn tires, because wear shrinks the circumference of the tire), vehicle manufacturers *intentionally* display slightly less than the speed that the equipment registers.

But generally, under "average" travel conditions, the lookup charts as well as the travel time maps will provide a reasonable estimate.

Ratio scales 

A map of an individual state may be scaled to fit the page or folding-map size. USGS topographical maps are available in a handful of specific scale sizes.

In this example, a scale of **1 : 126,720** may seem a crazy choice, but 2 miles = 5280 feet x 2. With 12 inches per foot,
$$5280 \textbf{ x } 2 \textbf{ x } 12 = 126{,}720$$
so on a map of this scale, 1 inch = 2 miles.

Bar scales 

A bar scale is usually shown in the legend of every map. It's use is simple. Lay your index finger (or a twig or toothpick) along the bar scale, and use the tip of your thumb to mark 1 mile or any other distance on the scale (say, 5 miles on this example). Then move that finger or twig along the road, and add up the distance. It will give you a rough estimate, since it ignores small curves in the road.

Marked distance between points 

On the newer map (2019), distance in miles is shown as a **BLACK** number between each road intersection to the next (or to the next town)--the blue arrows. The larger distance show in RED is the mileage between the two tiny red arrow points.

The older 1984 map of the same area shows only the short distances, and is missing roads that were added over the past 35 years.

Mileage lookup chart 

These can be rectangular, in which you look up one city on the right side of the chart, and the other along the top. Where the row and the column intersect shows the mileage.

They can also be triangular, like this one. Find the two desired city names, then see the mileage where the row from one intersects with the column of the other. Stillwater, Oklahoma to Tulsa is 64 miles.

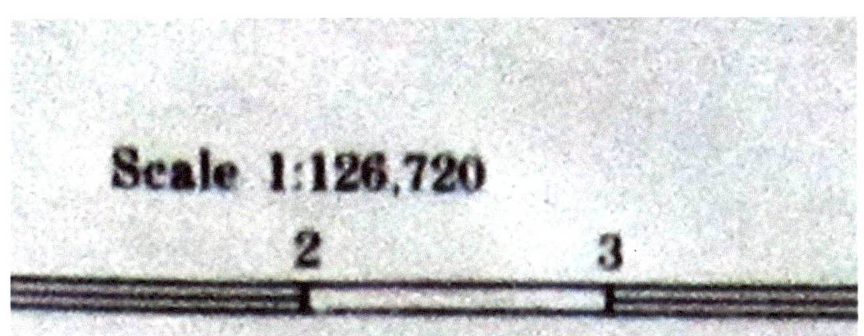

Scale 1:126,720
2
3

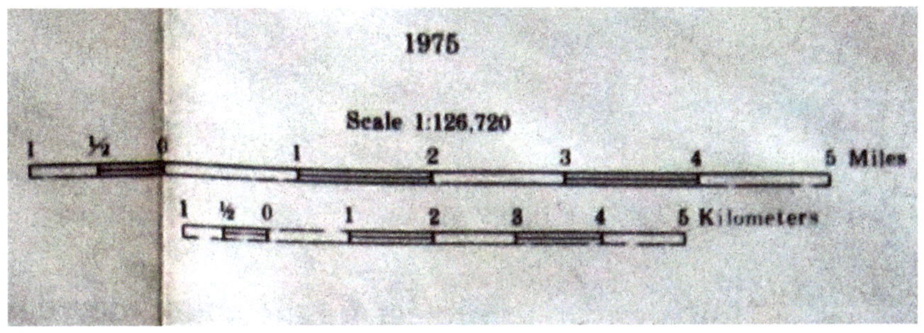

1975
Scale 1:126,720
1 ½ 0 1 2 3 4 5 Miles
1 ½ 0 1 2 3 4 5 Kilometers

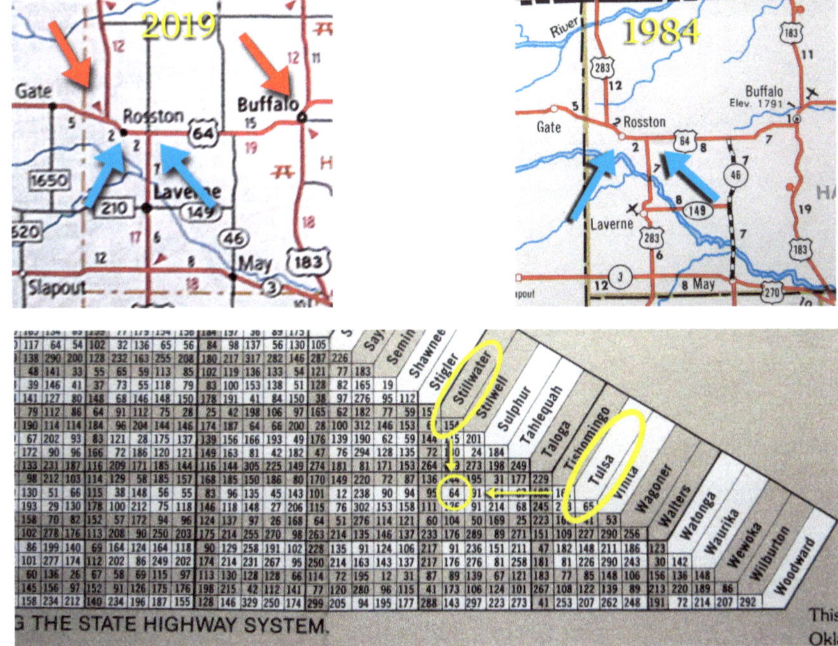

2019
Gate
Rosston
Buffalo
64
Laverne
149
1650
210
520
46
May
183
12
Slapout

1984
River
283
12
Gate
Rosston
64
46
149
Buffalo
Elev. 1791
183
283
Laverne
3
12
8 May
270
183
19
H

Sayr
Semin
Shawnee
Stigler
Stillwater
Stilwell
Sulphur
Tahlequah
Taloga
Tishomingo
Tulsa
Vinita
Wagoner
Walters
Watonga
Waurika
Wewoka
Wilburton
Woodward

G THE STATE HIGHWAY SYSTEM.
This
Okl

Map Insets

This state map includes inset maps of several cities. The inset map (below) contains its own inset of the Capitol Complex.

Extensions

In the main map below, the state line (diagonal yellow) between Virginia and Kentucky extends to a little corner, where West Virginia abuts them both. Since the square map won't fit that extra corner, the extension (the smaller map inset) really belongs at the position of the upper red 'A'. It's a Virginia map, so the extension inset simply hides part of Kentucky.

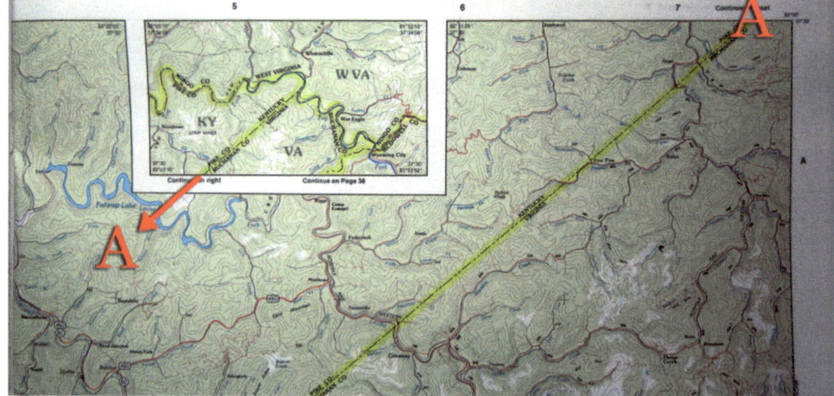

City Maps

City maps are often jammed with dense information. Streets are closely spaced, individually named, and sometimes even provided with ranges of street addresses for each block. Major buildings may be identified, cloverleaf entrances and exits to highways may be shown in fine detail. Significant sites, such as cemeteries, city parks, creeks, bridges and tunnels may be marked with symbols or contrasting shading.

The initial challenge in reading a city map of an unfamiliar city is to locate where you presently are (or expect to enter the city), and to locate your destination point. Using the map's index and its coordinates (horizontal and vertical, along the margins of the map) may make this easier.

Observe the map symbols for one-way streets. Keep in mind that following residential streets is nearly always slower than driving along major roads, even if those apparent "shortcuts" are tempting. Driving during weekday "rush hours" in the morning and early evening may prove frustrating.

Some city maps may show popular businesses, museums, sports venues, houses of worship and even restaurants. But if you are looking for a non-tourist business, such as a laundromat, you will likely have to ask a local resident for directions. (Looking up addresses in the phone book of a convenient pay phone is seldom an option any longer, since the widespread ownership of cell phones has made pay phones unprofitable to maintain in many locations.)

If you need to stop and ask directions in a large city, it is safest to do so in a location with many people, such as at a shopping center.

Bike paths and footpaths may or may not be marked on a city map. You may need to refer to a specialty map or tourist map to find their intersections with roads.

Likewise many city maps no longer clearly show city bus routes and stops, commuter rail stations (subway and elevated trains) or other means of public transportation. Specialty maps of these do exist, but you may have to ask where to obtain them.

Street names and street address numbers 
On some highly detailed city maps, the range of street address numbers may be shown for each city block. But most maps don't have this.

The road sign shown here says, "Dairy Rd. 3300". The "3300" is the beginning of the street address numbers at that *end* of the street. In most areas, even number addresses appear only on one *side* of the street, and odd numbers on the opposite side.

One-way streets 
The arrows marked over city streets usually indicate that these are one-way streets, moving in the direction the arrow is pointing. Navigating one-way streets within a city may require you to go around the block to reach a particular address. Road signs may warn you not to turn into a one-way street heading in the wrong direction. Carelessly making such a turn, and facing all lanes of traffic coming toward you is a sobering experience.

Public transit routes 
Some roadmaps may show the locations of bus lines or commuter rail service. This example from Chicago marks distinctive rail lines with different colors, and displays an icon at each stop as well as the train station. Don't count on finding this information on many city maps.

On foot or bike 
Cities and towns may have developed improved or paved trails intended for hiking or biking or both. Sometimes these are shown on city maps.

While dedicated bike lanes on roads are usually well marked on the pavement, and with road signs, they are often not shown on city maps. Some areas have laws requiring your vehicle to maintain a certain distance from bikes traveling in bike lanes.

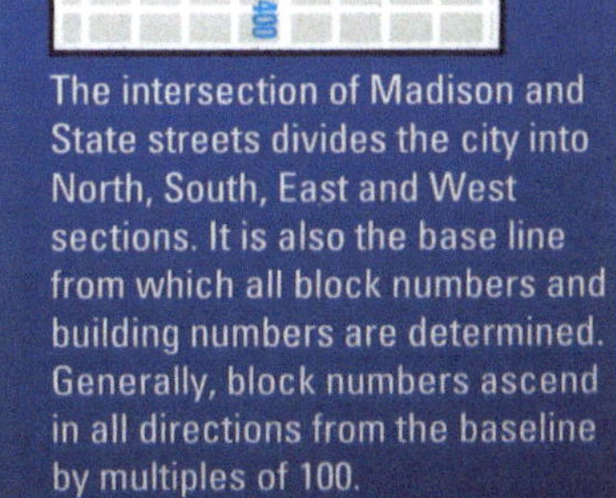

The intersection of Madison and State streets divides the city into North, South, East and West sections. It is also the base line from which all block numbers and building numbers are determined. Generally, block numbers ascend in all directions from the baseline by multiples of 100.

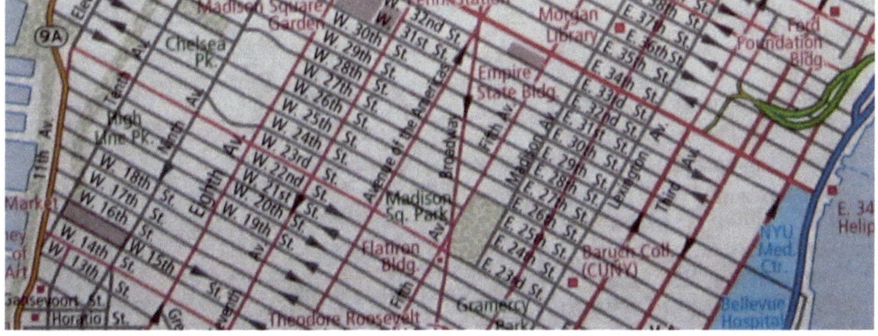

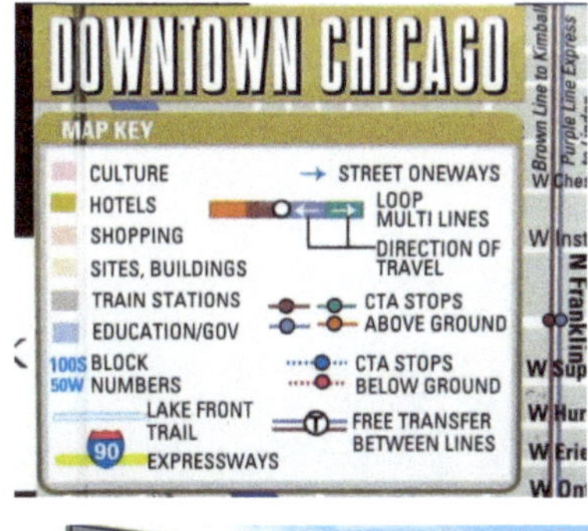

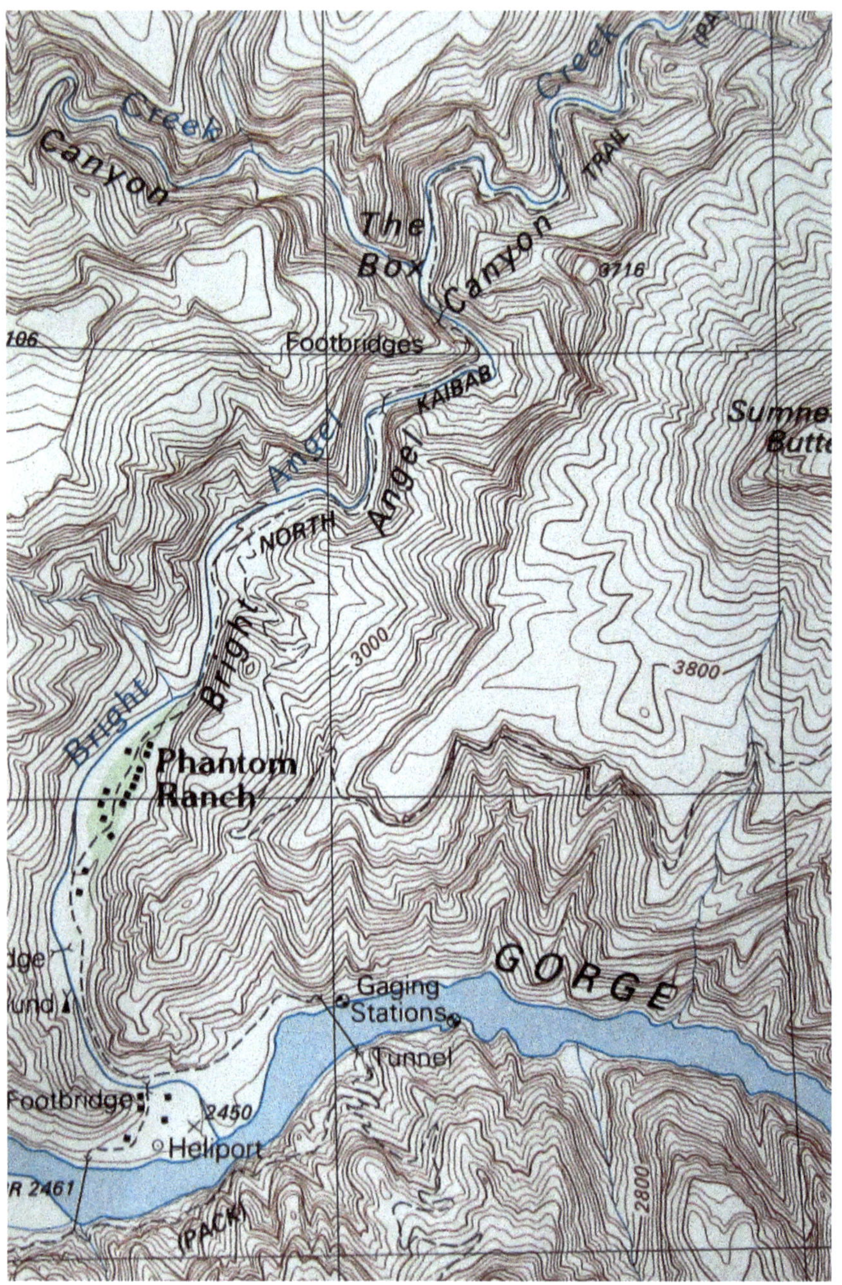

The tiny, black squares shown at Phantom Ranch represent individual, small buildings. Two hiker and equine bridges (fine black lines) are shown crossing the Colorado River.

County and Topographical Roadmaps

A map dedicated to an individual county will include most secondary roads, some gravel roads, and sometimes even dirt roads. Details of urban areas may be skimpy. These come as "flat" maps, which ignore the terrain, or as topographical (topo) maps, which include contour lines to indicate differences in elevation and the grade of slopes.

Dedicated topo maps are not primarily roadmaps, but include every detail that is possible to include on maps of each scale. Major roads are shown on topo maps of all scales. The least improved roads and trails (dirt roads, hiking trails, driveways) will appear on the most detailed of these. Individual structures are marked with symbols, and carefully drawn contours offer the clearest picture of elevation, slope and grade.

The US Geological Survey (USGS) has mapped every part of the US. Maps are available from them directly:

https://store.usgs.gov/maps

This website offers maps in a range of sizes and scales, as well as a number of types of specialty maps. Their map scales are stated in "minutes" (60 minutes = 1 degree of latitude or longitude), so a 7.5 minute map covers a *smaller area* than a 15 minute map. A 7.5 minute map is therefore *more detailed* than a 15 minute map of the same region. USGS provides the mapping for National Forests and National Parks.

Select USGS maps are available at various backcountry outfitters and some bookstores and Park visitor centers.

Because of their fine level of detail, USGS maps may show roads that are so primitive or literally unmaintained that they are not passable by most vehicles, even high-clearance four-wheel drive vehicles. Based on the line type used to depict the road, carefully judge its likely quality by looking at the road types in the map's key.

Despite these concerns, your best bet for seeing what roads exist in National Parks, National Forests, and other federal lands is a well-chosen USGS map. But be smart about which roads you chose to follow.

Paved vs. unpaved roads 

Paved roads are usually passable in all but the most troublesome weather conditions. Unpaved roads may quickly become impassable with even modest rain or snow.

While many unpaved roads are unpaved from end to end, some paved roads may abruptly change to unpaved roads as you drive along. A reliable map should indicate this. The asphalt road in the image abruptly transitions to a gravel road.

Topographical map vs. roadmap 

These two maps attempt to show Grand Canyon Village. The roadmap (right) provides enough detail to allow you to find Grand Canyon Village when you drive there. The topo map (left) is so detailed that you can actually identify individual water tanks (round black objects) and buildings (rectangular black objects), as well as every gravel road loop within Mather Campground. The Visitor Center is marked on both.

Dubious roads 

If you are just cruising around in a remote area, with no particular destination other than seeing the countryside, be wary of deteriorated road conditions. The partly washed-out road in the image is currently passable. If rain resumes, it may become impassable. Some unimproved roads can present a challenge if you should need to turn around, because of their narrow, single lane, and the absence of a safe road shoulder. Learn to perform a *tight* 3-point turn.

Contour lines

The squiggly brown lines are known as contour lines. Their purpose is to show elevation. This map's legend (not shown) tells us that each line indicates 40 feet of elevation change. The darker brown lines indicate 200 feet of change. The actual elevation of particular dark lines is shown on other areas of the map. The river is at 2400 feet (above sea level). The foot trail is at about 3700 feet. So the cliff from the foot trail to the river is a 1300 foot drop.

unpaved
paved

Central Grand
Canyon N.P.
Point Imperial
8803 ft.
NAVAJO
NATION
NORTH
North Rim
Vis. Ctr.
Cape Royal Rd.
Cape Solitude
6144 ft.
Pt. Sublime
7459 ft.
Grand Canyon Lodge
Bright Angel Pt.
8145 ft.
Cottonwood
Ribbon Falls
RIM
KAIBAB TRAIL
Walhalla
Overlook
Yavapai Pt.
Overlook & Bright
Geology Mus. Angel
Phantom Ranch
Cape Royal
7865 ft.
Ranger Sta.
EAST RIM
SOUTH
Indian Gdn.
Mather Pt. Overlook/
Vis. Ctr.
Desert View
Hermits
Rest
Hermit
Rd.
Yaki Pt. Overlook
The Watchtower
Grand Canyon
Village
RIM
Grandview Pt.
Overlook
Desert View
E. ENTRANCE
STA. (FEE)
S. ENTRANCE
STA. (FEE)
Ranger
Sta.
Desert
View
Dr.
Tusayan
Ruin &
Mus.
Grand Canyon
N.P. Arpt.
Tusayan
ARIZ.
NAT'L SCENIC TR.
KAIBAB
N.F.
© Rand McN.

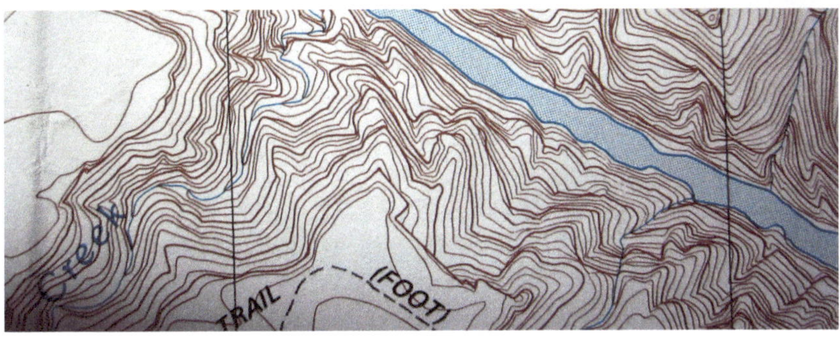
Creek
TRAIL (FOOT)

If you need to pull over to read a roadmap, find a safe place.

US Highway and Interstate Maps

State maps and regional maps (like the South-East US) are primarily designed to allow you to easily drive long distances. They will always show Interstate highways, US highways, toll roads (which may also be Interstate highways), and State highways. Smaller roads, such as county roads, may not appear at all.

It is possible, for example, to start out on Interstate 40 in Wilmington, North Carolina, on the Atlantic Ocean, and drive as far west as Barstow, California, still on I-40. Likewise I-10 can take you from Jacksonville, Florida to Los Angeles. I-80 runs from New York City to the San Francisco Bay. While such 3000 mile trips are certainly an exception, it demonstrates the simplicity of planning some very long routes within the US.

There are also Interstate highways and US highways that run North-to-South, as well as diagonally through major portions of the country. A road atlas of the US can allow you to plan both long and short trips.

Rest areas are positioned at various intervals (20 to 50 or more miles apart) along the Interstate highways. These may be as simple as a parking area with restrooms, or provide picnic tables beneath shelters, and a selection of snack and beverage vending machines. Some have staffed information desks, and even gift shops.

These rest areas are managed by the states in which they are located, and are sometimes closed for maintenance or because of restricted state budgets.

On maps of larger regions, the number of different symbols, line colors and line widths (designating different types of roads) may be large. So examining the map *legend* may be helpful.

If your route passes through a major city without any need to stop there, look for bypasses (or circumferential Interstates), which are usually designated with a 3 digit route number. Avoiding city traffic can save a lot of travel time.

Once you leave an Interstate highway, you may or may not need a more detailed, local map to continue to your destination.

Rest Areas and Picnic Areas 

The reason rest areas exist on Interstate highways is so that you can plan on bathroom breaks (and maybe a snack) without the need to exit the Interstate and locate a commercial establishment, such as a gas station, in order to use the restroom. Rest areas are announced on large road signs well in advance of them. The rest areas may have separate parking for cars and large trucks, and they often have picnic tables available beneath shelters. Two rest areas are shown on the map (blue icons).

Mile Markers and Exit Numbers 

Interstate highways display small or large "mile markers" at least every mile, and often small ones every tenth of a mile. You can use these, together with a timer or the second hand on a watch to test the accuracy of your speedometer. These same mile numbers are used to label exits. So in the example, Exits 105 and 132 are also mile markers, from the start of the road in that state. Knowing your location to the nearest mile marker can assist emergency responders, should you or others need assistance.

City bypasses 

Interstate highways that pass through major and medium-size cities provide an alternative route for through traffic, so drivers can avoid congested traffic (especially during rush hours). I-40 passes through the middle of Nashville. I-840 is a lazy loop to the south, that eventually connects back to I-40 west of the city. That bypass is nearly always faster than the direct route, except during the middle of the night, when there is little city traffic.

Toll roads 

Toll roads are indicated by a different color line (in this case, a green line). Fees on toll roads vary by state. There are usually no free Interstate roads that follow the same general path as a toll road, so there is not much choice about which type of road to take. Just plan the fees you'll need to pay.

In this example, the Pennsylvania Turnpike (I-76) goes east to west, while I-81 drops south into Virginia and Tennessee.

730
Blacksburg
785 | Mill
132 24
Smithfield Plantation
McCoy
Parrott
Belspring
Prices
Fork
Va. Polytechnic Inst. and St. Univ.
Ironto
Dixie
Lafayette
Elliston
Fairlawn
114
Radford Univ.
627
Shawsville
81
Alleghany Spring
Radford
105
19
Christiansburg

730
Blacksburg
785 | Mill
132 24
Smithfield Plantation
McCoy
Parrott
Belspring
Prices
Fork
Va. Polytechnic Inst. and St. Univ.
Ironto
Dixie
Lafayette
Elliston
Fairlawn
114
Radford Univ.
627
Shawsville
81
Alleghany Spring
Radford
105
19
Christiansburg

Nashville, TN
Green Hill
Mount Juliet
Leeville
Lebanon
Carthage
Grant 5
201
226
239
Shop Springs
40
New Middleton
840
Bairds Mill
Commerce
Forest Hills
Long Hunter S.P.
J. Percy Priest L.
Nashville Int'l
Gladeville
Watertown
Main Interstate
Oak Hill
24
231
Alexandria
Norene
257
Liberty
41
70S
La Vergne
Smyrna
452
Brentwood
74 11 59
Silverhill
266
Greenvale
Berrys Chapel
397
66
65
Aubentown
Milton
Franklin
96
Bypass
65
ALT 41 ALT 31
Sam Davis Home
Walterhill
Leipers Fork
Nolensville
57
Lascassas
53
Gassaw
Clovercroft
STONES RIVER NAT'L B'LD.
CANNON
252
Triune
Almaville
96
Shiloh
Burwood
Arrington
42
Peytonsville
96
Kittrell
Readyville
Woodbury
Murfreesboro
Middle Tenn.

997
25
76
Mechanicsburg
Carlisle Barracks
KITTATINNY TUN.
201
Greason
44
Shepherdstow
47
Newville
61
533
37
31
465
Boiling Springs
Allen
McKinney
BLUE
Toll Road
Newburg
11
CUMBERLAND
Brandtsville
Roxbury
Oakville
Dickinson
Mt. Holly Sprs.
Mowersville
Lurgan
Middle Spring
Stoughstown
174
Huntsdale
Beavertown
997
Kings Gap Env. Ed. Ctr.
Franklintown
Pleasant Hall
Mongul
Orrstown
Shippensburg Univ.
Walnut Bottom
Brushtown
Hunts Run
No Toll
Shippensburg
29
Lees Cross Roads
233
Grove
Furnace
Goodyear
York Springs
Clear Spring
Nyesville
Pinola
81
24
Cleversburg
TRAIL
MICHAUX

Tourist Maps

Tourist maps are offered for most popular tourist destinations. They are sometimes made for local or regional government tourism bureaus. These will emphasize popular sites and areas.

By contrast, tourist maps developed and paid for by commercial advertisers (specific businesses in the area) may focus on those particular businesses.

Regardless of their source, tourist maps are often not drawn to scale, should not be relied upon as roadmaps, and should only be used to *suggest* things and places to see.

Advertisements

Each ad surrounding this map has an index number to match the location of that business on the map itself.

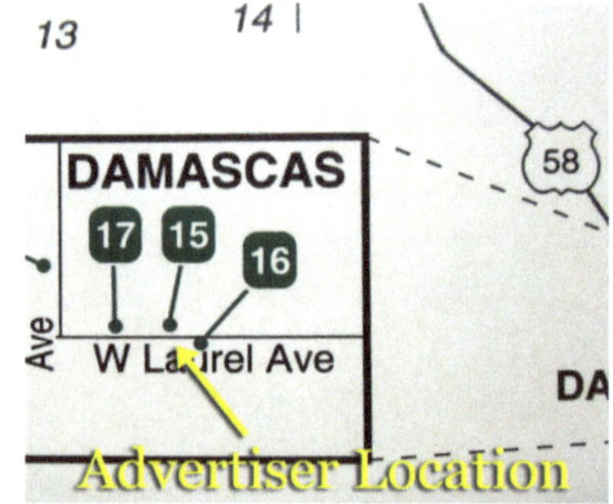

Forest Service Maps

Some fairly large areas in some parts the US are occupied by National and State Forests, wildlife preserves, and wilderness areas. The Forest Service manages private and commercial tree cutting within its forests. So logging "trails"—infrequently maintained, poorly graded, dirt or gravel roads—are common. And they appear on Forest Service maps.

Before you venture onto a remote forest service road, be sure to let someone know where you plan to go, and when you expect to return. Also choose the season and weather conditions carefully.

Forest Service roads may offer the only vehicle access to some regions. But to take advantage of them, you may need four-wheel drive and a high clearance vehicle. If you decide on such an adventure, bring along extra food and water, and clothing suitable for any possible weather conditions. Cell phone service may be completely absent.

Forests host a wide variety of wildlife that you may encounter on the road. This can range from deer to elk to moose to grizzly bears. Since many parcels of national land are sometimes leased to ranchers for grazing, you may also find cattle or sheep. While each of these presents its own special danger, they can also appear as unexpected road hazards. Any wildlife other than grazing livestock should be regarded as wild and potentially dangerous.

If you intend to leave your vehicle, and hike or camp away from the Forest Service road, park so as to not block the road. Don't leave food in the vehicle, since certain larger animals may damage it in an effort to obtain the food that they can easily smell.

When you finish such an excursion, be sure to check-in again with whomever you informed about your plans and your expected return date and time.

Lack of signs 

Roads through remote areas, such as desert or mountains or forests may or may not have an identifying road sign where it intersects with a highway, but seldom have signs farther into the area. Other roads that intersect with it may bear no road sign. Only a reliable roadmap of the area (and a compass) can solve the puzzle of a '**Y**' fork that is not marked by a sign. Getting lost in such a location can be life-threatening, if you are not prepared with extra food and water. Cell phone coverage is poor.

Infrequent maintenance 

This is part of the symbol key for a USGS map of the Badlands National Park, in South Dakota. If we ignore the worrisome sound of the name, "Badlands", the key itself gives us a sense of the quality of the roads. The third from the top includes "hard *or improved surface*". So these may be gravel or maintained dirt roads. The next one down, "**Other road**", is not as good as that, or is not maintained frequently enough to assure passage of a passenger vehicle (or any vehicle).

Is it passable? 

Unmaintained roads do get maintained, but not very often. Gravel and dirt surfaces are usually impassable after a modest snowfall or sometimes after a modest rain storm. Some turn to quagmires, with two-foot-deep mud holes that appear at first glance to be simple puddles. Heavy rains may wash away portions of a road that cross a natural creek bed, even when a culvert pipe has been installed. Exposed rocks can destroy the undercarriage of a car, or puncture a gas tank or engine oil pan.

Middle of nowhere 

Be aware of how remote your destination may be from other people and access to assistance. USGS maps often show many poorly maintained "roads" into wilderness and deserts and mountains and forests. If your car or truck should have a problem in one of these locations, there may be no cell phone towers, no passing traffic, no nearby people and no available food or water. Sudden weather changes may also be a challenge.

?

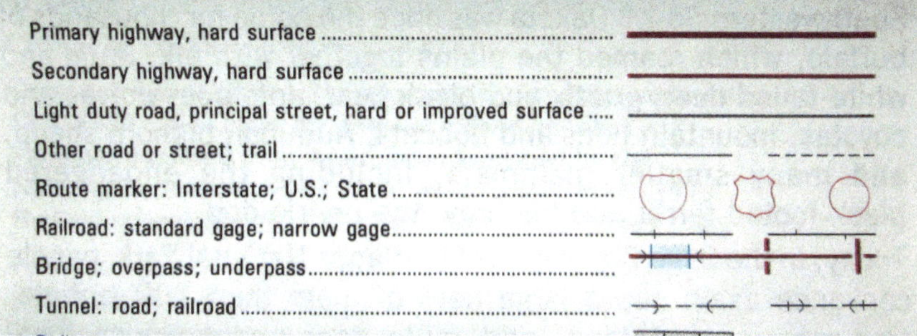
Primary highway, hard surface
Secondary highway, hard surface
Light duty road, principal street, hard or improved surface
Other road or street; trail
Route marker: Interstate; U.S.; State
Railroad: standard gage; narrow gage
Bridge; overpass; underpass
Tunnel: road; railroad

These signs pass by quickly. The more cities listed, the more difficult it is to read the mileage that may interest you.

Estimating Driving Time

An obvious reason for estimating your driving time is to know when you need to depart, in order to arrive at your destination near a particular time. For longer drives, estimating driving time allows you to plan in advance for driver swaps (if more than one of you is driving), rest breaks, and reasonable points at which to stop for the night—so you can book a motel in advance.

It's certainly possible to drive 15 or 16 hours in a day, but this requires getting enough sleep prior to your departure, and taking frequent (every 2 to 3 hours) breaks, in order to refresh your mind and your muscles. In attempting to drive for long hours in a day, don't wait to become drowsy before stopping at a rest area to catch a brief nap.

Be realistic in planning your distances for a long drive. As an example, a 2000 mile trip, say from the southeast US to Arizona, driven at 70 mph, computes to 29 hours total driving time. But with breaks and meals, this time balloons to nearly 40 hours. That's a work week of driving, over less than two days. This can be successfully done with 3 or 4 drivers taking turns during the drive. A single driver will simply need one or two good nights of sleep in route.

Hurrying to reach a wonderful destination seems like a good plan. But don't forget that a meaningful part of every special trip or vacation is the journey there and back. It is easy to focus too much on rapid travel, while missing out on the joys of traveling.

Air travel has accustomed many travelers to regard the long stretches of the US that they *fly over* as not worth visiting. Each region of the US possesses its own beauty, charms and treasures.

When you estimate driving times, feel free to include extra time for seeing more of what you would otherwise zoom past. Remember that a roadmap shows you not only your origin and destination, but all the possibilities in between. It's one of the benefits of a printed map.

Indicated travel times 

Some maps and road atlases include estimated driving times between points. These driving times are not usually just the distance divided by the speed limit. The estimated driving time may take into account the steepness of the terrain, the average traffic burden and other factors that might slow down your driving. The travel time in this illustration between Amarillo, TX and Tucumcari, NM is stated as 1 hour and 44 minutes, even though the distance of 112 miles, traveling at the 70 mph speed limit is only 1 hour and 36 minutes.

These estimated driving times should be regarded as merely rough guides, and are often most useful in comparing two or more alternative routes between the same locations. As you can see from the "map", the connecting lines may not identify particular highways, but rather the "best" routes between two points. You'll have to consult the roadmap to find the roads.

Long drive 50 mph estimate 

In viewing routes for longer drives, the same issues apply. In this example, we are looking at the drive between Roanoke, VA and Birmingham, AL. The driving time "map" presents two likely paths between those cities. By totaling the miles of each segment of a path, and totaling the time of each segment, we can easily see that the path that passes through Knoxville and Chattanooga, TN is both shorter in distance and faster than going through Asheville, NC and Atlanta, GA.

But are we really expecting to drive 8-1/2 hours non-stop? Taking a break at least once every couple of hours is common. These breaks may be at rest areas, for meals, or for fuel. A useful rule of thumb for estimating the *total time* for a long distance drive is to pretend you are driving straight through, but at **50 mph**, in order to include time for breaks. So our example 8-1/2 hour drive, but taking ~10 hours, allows an hour for a meal plus two 15 minute rest stops.

Miles
Tucumcari 112
Amarillo
1:44
Driving Time

Driving Times/Distan
Actual travel times may va

518 miles, Quicker Route ~8-1/2 hours
587 miles, Slower Route ~10 hours

     Robert C.A. Goff

Using a Map While Driving

A roadmap is most useful for driving, but looking at a roadmap while driving can be dangerous. If you can inspect the part of the map you need to see in less than two or three seconds, that is usually not a problem on a road with little traffic.

In heavy or close traffic, those few seconds of distraction may be enough to cause a collision—possibly at high speed. So make every effort to *not need to look at the map* on congested roads.

One approach to minimizing your need to inspect the map is to prepare in advance. Plan your route, and mark your map. Make abbreviated written instructions on a separate piece of paper. Note the route numbers and important turns or changes of highways, and perhaps the estimated mileage between each of your route changes.

If you've done your best to prepare in advance, but still find yourself confused along a particular stretch of the journey, then safely pull off the road. If there is a rest area, park there to study your map. If not, then pull completely onto the right shoulder of the road, stop, then look at your map.

Truck stops are often a helpful place to ask for directions. If you know that you will be approaching a major city with a confusion of multiple Interstate and US highways crisscrossing in multiple directions, stop before you get there, and either clarify in your own mind where you need to go (and hopefully clarify your brief, written notes), or ask someone for directions.

If you do need to ask for directions, do so with your map in your hand. That visual aid will improve the reliability of the answer you get, and will firm it in your mind more effectively than repeating verbal instructions to yourself.

Be safe. Arrive late, rather than not at all.

Advanced preparation   

Mark your route with a highlighter. This will be easy to see, yet will not cover up any of the tiny details and symbols on a map. Then, with a dark pen, mark arrows indicating turns and changes of highways. Write the exit number and route number large enough to easily spot without having to stare at the map.

For short legs of a trip that require multiple turns onto different secondary roads, marking the mileage between turns may help in identifying those turns as you approach them. Try to keep your separate, written notes of routes and turns as brief and legible as possible.

When to pull over   

The Interstate highway approaches to major cities can be confusing. Exits are more numerous and closer together. Many other Interstates may be intersecting in quick succession. If you are unfamiliar with the area, marking your route in advance might be helpful. Also, a brief list of exit numbers and turns could be useful. But you can't look at either of these for more than two or three seconds while on the move. Doing so is just too dangerous. The safest alternative is to just pull off the road safely—at a rest area or even an exit. Study the map carefully, then return to your route.

Asking directions with your map in hand   

Sometimes you've just got to ask. Asking a stranger for directions is always an exercise in trusting the knowledge and good will of fellow humans.

When you do need to ask directions, carry a map that you can show to your stranger. Request that he or she point out the turns and the destination. The directions may still be incorrect, but that is less likely to lead you astray than a list of how many traffic lights you should count. Ask for a landmark at each recommend turn. "Be sure to turn left at the building that used to be the Tastee Freeze."

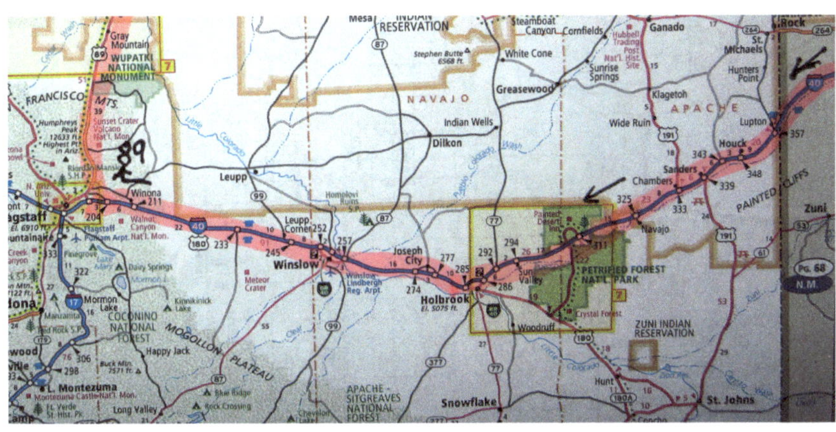

Chicago
DUPAGE
COOK
Univ. of Illinois at Chicago
Univ. of Chicago
Naperville
Aurora
Joliet

TRUCK DIESEL
EXXON
BUMP
BUMP